This book belongs to:

_____

_____

This is a work of fiction. Any resemblance to actual persons, living or dead, events or locales is entirely coincidental.

Text and Illustrations Copyright © Dave Whittle 2023

Illustrations by Kris Lillyman 2023

Moral rights asserted

The right of Dave Whittle and Kris Lillyman to be identified as the Author and Illustrator of this work has been asserted by them in accordance with the Copyright, Design and Patents Act 1988.

All rights reserved. No part of this publication may be reproduced, stored in a retrieval system, or transmitted, in any form, or by any means (electronic, mechanical, photocopying, recording or otherwise) without the prior written permission of the publisher.

Dave Whittle

Pirates Rule Okay!

Illustrated by Kris Lillyman

Now who, you may wonder, be Barnabas Bligh?
A world-famous pirate, no word of a lie,
You'll hear of his tale of brave deeds soon enough,
He's fearless, he's tireless and made of stern stuff!

A seafaring legend, a seeker of treasure,
And plunderin' booty, his main source of pleasure.
He captains a ship, that can rule all the waves,
He's sent many folks to their watery graves.

He wears a black eye patch, that covers one eye,
And tells many tales to explain reasons why.
Some say these be fake, for heroic appeal,
Yet nobody knows if for sure they be real.

PIRATES RULE OKAY!

WANTED FOR PIRACY
CAP'N BARNABAS BLIGH
REWARD

YE OLDE PAINT

He met with a smuggler, who gave him a map,
An' sly Smuggler Sam be a crafty old chap.
He wanted a slice of reward from this trade,
So, Bligh, he agreed, and a fair deal was made.

So, this be a tale of a brave treasure quest,
At seeking out treasure, he's one of the best.
But one thing is missing from Cap'n Bligh's life,
And that be the love of a good pirate wife.

No longer to keep you all there in suspense,
Turn over the page, let the story commence.

In fine Cornish coves, where the caves meet the sea,
You'll find that's where smugglers and pirates roam free.
Takes all sorts to join in these dark, shady ways,
A life of adventure - a good job that pays!

These ladies no longer need wear their posh frocks,
They've trained in bad deeds and have learned to pick locks.
So keen to find peril and earn their rewards,
To plunder and fight, and to fence with their swords.

Their lives had been boring and no fun at all,
They fled from their homes and have answered the call.
To sign up and sail with the brave pirate men,
In search of a thrill, to be happy again.

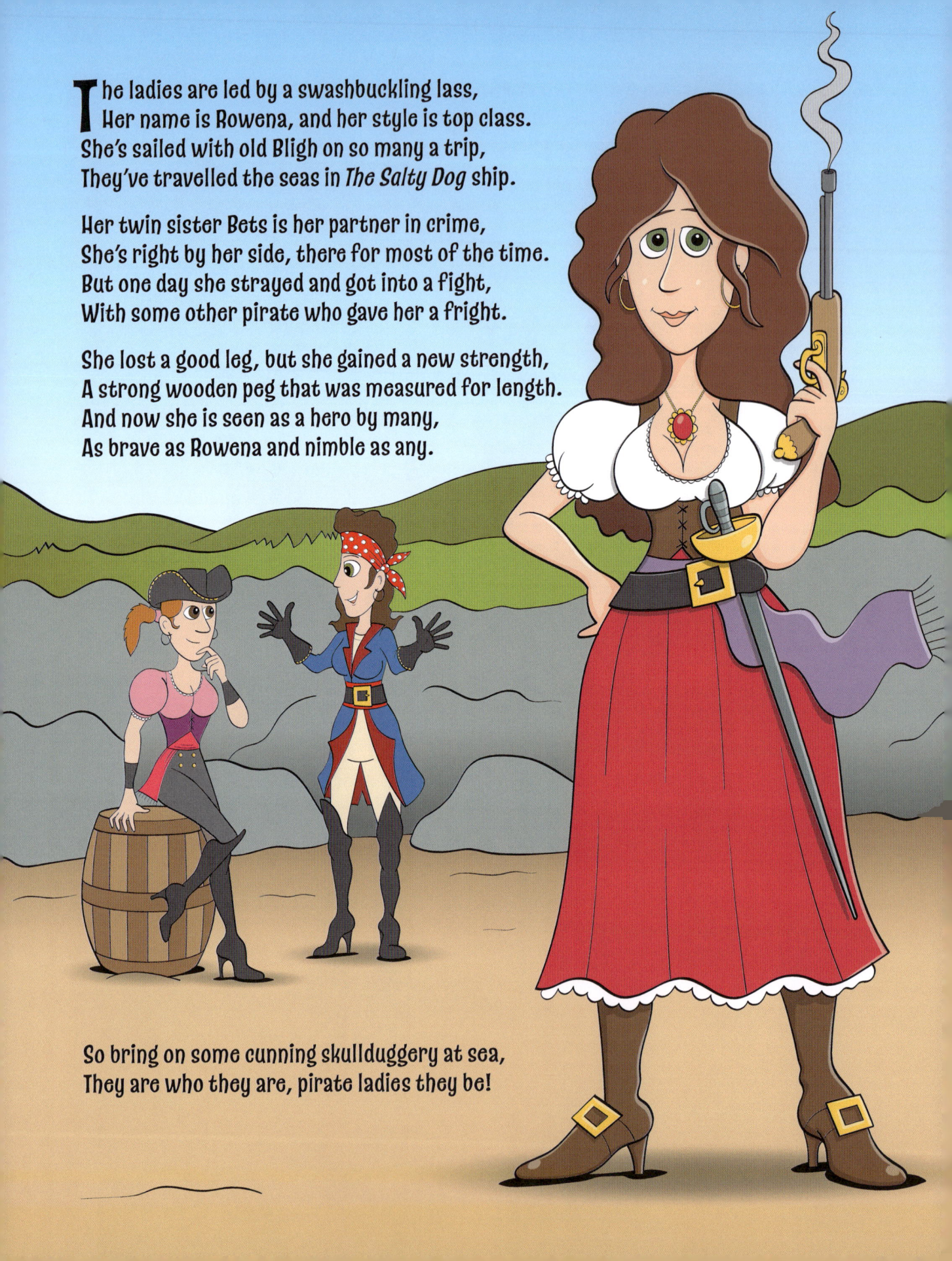

The ladies are led by a swashbuckling lass,
Her name is Rowena, and her style is top class.
She's sailed with old Bligh on so many a trip,
They've travelled the seas in *The Salty Dog* ship.

Her twin sister Bets is her partner in crime,
She's right by her side, there for most of the time.
But one day she strayed and got into a fight,
With some other pirate who gave her a fright.

She lost a good leg, but she gained a new strength,
A strong wooden peg that was measured for length.
And now she is seen as a hero by many,
As brave as Rowena and nimble as any.

So bring on some cunning skullduggery at sea,
They are who they are, pirate ladies they be!

Sly Sam knows a secret about Captain Bligh,
He'd best get his prize, or he'll tell passers-by!
If truth e'er got out it would dent pirate pride,
No wonder it's something Bligh's wanting to hide.

But all he need do, is to bring back some gold,
Sam wants to have treasure to have and to hold.
Now, smuggling and blackmail are what Sam does best,
Let's hope that our cap'n be up to the test.

Sergeant Rob

Now up on the cliffs, where the coastguards hide out,
Upholding the law and of that there's no doubt.
They squat in the rain on the damp, English soil,
All soaked to the bone and yet on they still toil.

The wise Sergeant Rob, who with Crab and with Evans,
Placed hands on their hearts and then swore to the heavens.
"We're loyal and we serve both the country and crown,
We'll risk all our lives so that good folk don't drown".

Constable Evans

Constable Crab

And spyin' out pirates is part of their job,
On lookout for cut-throats or bandits that mob.
They peer through their scopes, so they'll know who deceives,
And leap out to catch all those rotters and thieves.

These pillars of justice all sing of their woes,
Their cape-wearing deeds and their thoughts on their foes.
They do like good weather but cope when it rains,
Relieving those rogues of their ill-gotten gains.

So, pirates and blaggards
and coastguards abound,
But still there is more
about Bligh to be found.
A big bearded man
with a wide cheeky grin,
A man you can warm to,
your heart he will win.
He's brave and he's loud
and his stature is tall,
Believes that he be,
the best pirate of all!

Ever since a young lad,
he has loved being at sea,
To sail the wide oceans
and be wild and free.
He went to the best
of the pirating schools,
Where all must be clever,
'twas no place for fools!

From deckhand and onwards to great master's mate,
A rise through the ranks would then make him first-rate.
He soon became boss, a brave captain so new,
Distinguished and loved by the rest of the crew.

He's proud of his crew and they all serve him well,
They all board the ship when he rings the ship's bell.
He'll speak of adventures, he's got one in mind,
Involving some treasure, he hopes they will find.

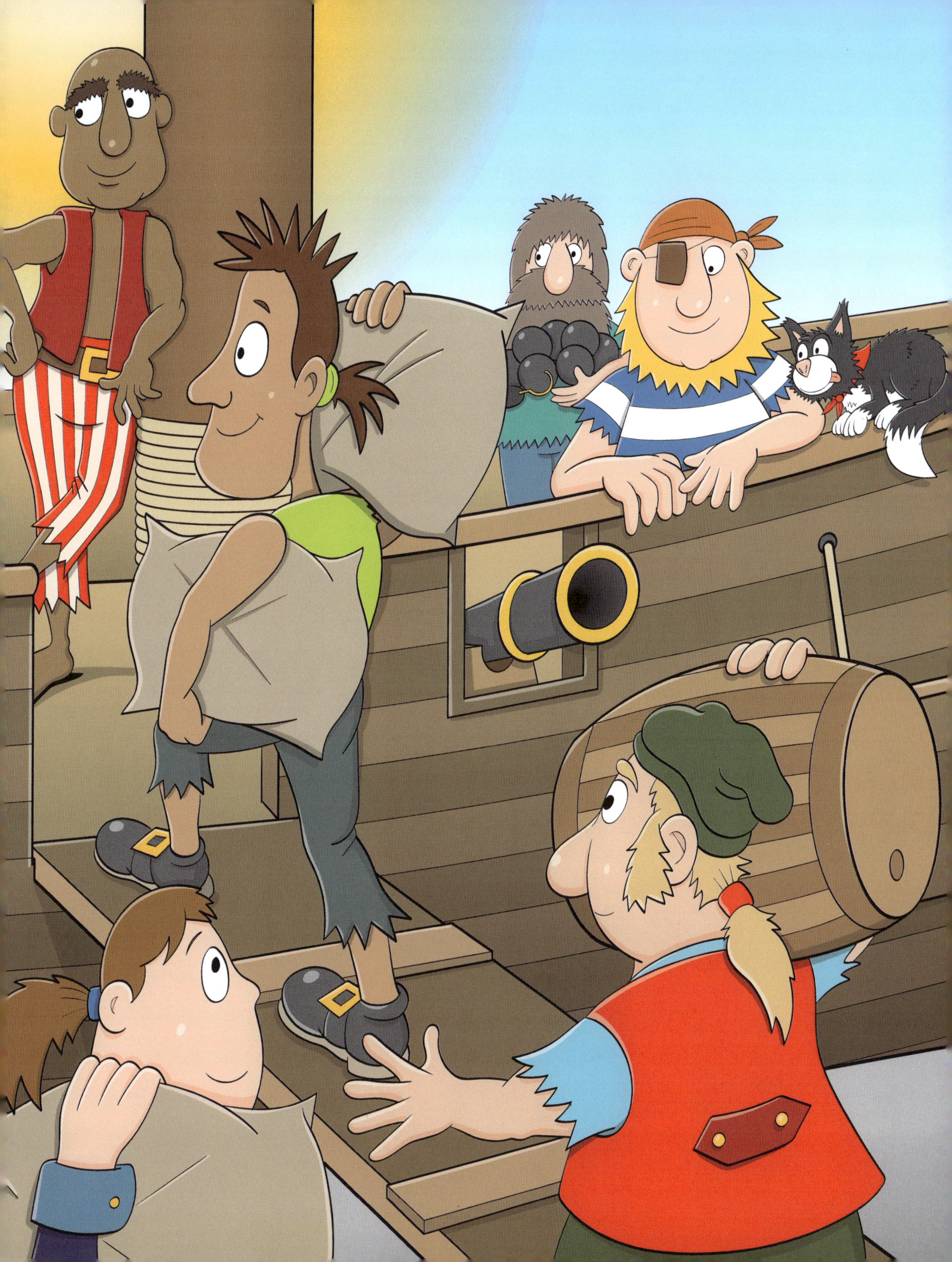

Before they can hear of this new, cunning plan,
A quick urgent message from ME, Pirate Stan!
"There's someone approaching in awful distress,
A young pirate lass in a royal blue dress."

A panicking Bets comes a-limping at speed,
With most awful news, that they must all now heed!

"The coastguards, they came and then captured Rowena,
They took all her money and her new concertina.
We must travel fast so she cannot confess,
If secrets are spilled, then we're all in a mess!"

OH HORROR!

They must free their crewmate,
some rescue plans made,
They gather their weapons,
prepare for a raid.

A much calmer Bets
now feels help is at hand,
The best pirate gang
that there be in the land!

Rowena is tied up
and held rather firm,
Whilst Rob tries to stop her
from trying to squirm.
But then she thinks hard
and comes up with a plan,
She'll charm
the soft sergeant
and that plan began!

So Bets tells old Bligh
of the best path to take,
And Bligh listens hard,
as so much is at stake.
The life of her sister,
her comrade and twin,
Bligh gathers his crew,
let the rescue begin!

The pirates take off
to save one of their own,
Old Bligh always wins
if the truth e'er be known.
But wait, there she is,
now all free from her chains,
They stare into space,
as they scratch out their brains.

Who stands right behind her?
The sergeant, who beams!
Rowena had spoken
of treasure that gleams.
If guards joined the pirates
to search for the gold,
They'd come back rich men,
and the deal was then sold.

With hopes and a dream of exceptional wages,
He freed all the pirates from dungeons and cages.
Now all on one team they can share the same aim,
Without any malice and no-one to blame.

Our Bligh is so pleased at what Rowena's done,
They meet in his room for a chat and some fun.
They find themselves laughing, enjoying their time,
To fall so in love...would it be such a crime?

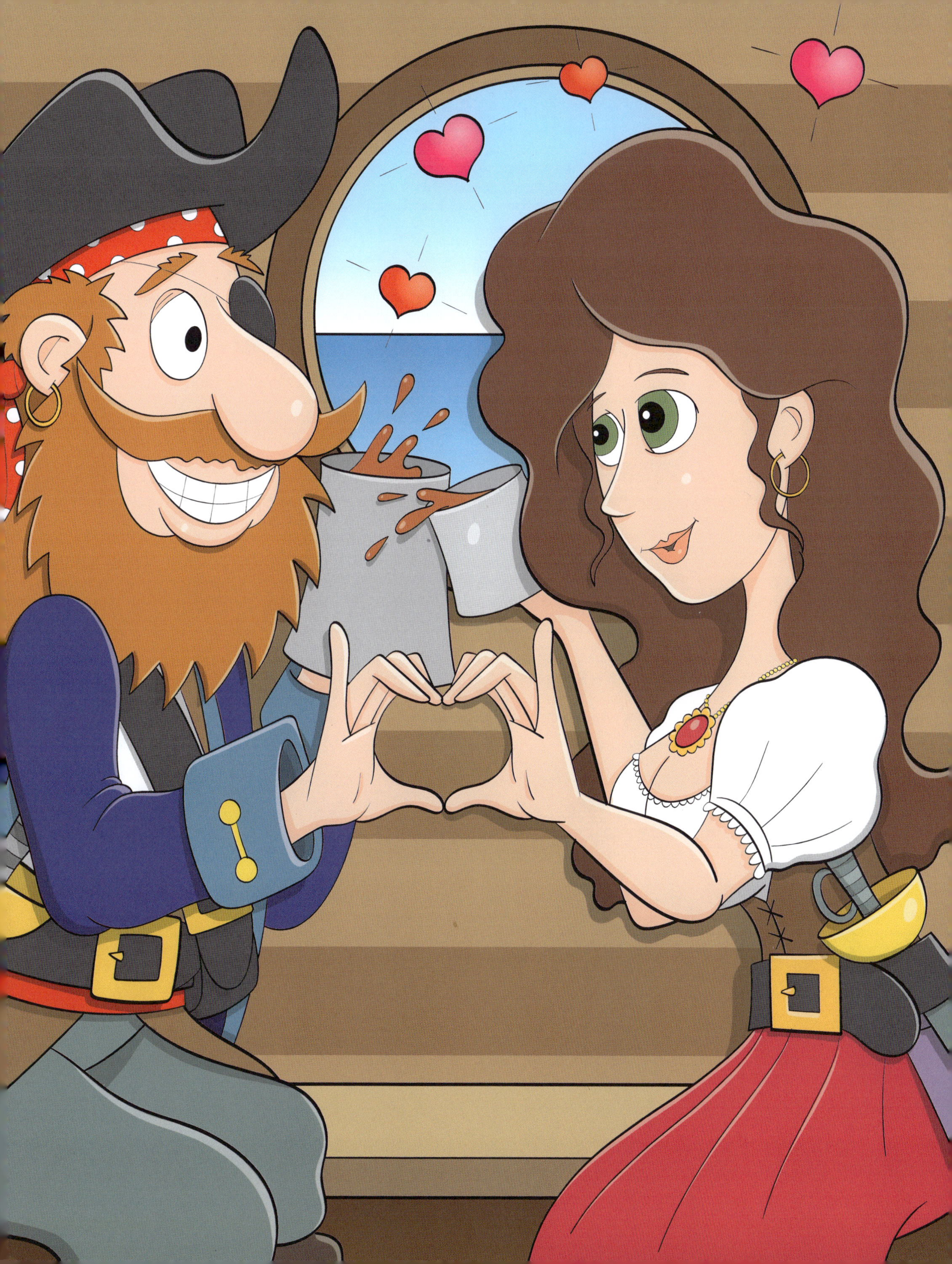

So now we all know that sweet love's in the air,
The ship be in harbour and weather be fair.
They'll hunt for doubloons, minted coins made of gold,
Or pieces-of-eight, made from silver, I'm told.

The crew go ashore,
they've been granted time off,
They want to go shopping
and snatch up some scoff!
Old Bligh stays behind, he can open the map,
To scope out the journey, look out for a trap.

PALM ISLAND
N
E
W
S
SHARKS!
Cut Throat Caves
Dead Man Falls
Mermaid Lagoon
WHALE BAY
TREASURE
Strange Statues
ROUGH SEAS

CRANIUM COVE

Pirate Peaks

Octopus Pass

Fire Mountain

Crocodile Creek

Mayan Ruins

WRECKAGE REEF

THE CAPTAIN'S EYE

SEA MONSTERS!

'Tis quite late at night and the inn lights shine bright,
The tavern be rowdy but no fight tonight.
There's whoopin' and cheerin' for what lies ahead,
But first they make merry, and with grub, are well fed.

Clay pipes give out stench and an unholy fog,
All tell of tall tales that are fuelled by some grog.

With clinking of tankard and goblet and jar,
Strong bonds they be sealed for their travels afar.

WANTED
CAP'N BLACKBEARD

This eve they all sing of the man they admire,
An' even the sergeant joins in with the choir.
At dawn on the morrow, it's time to set sail,
With Bligh at the helm, we all know they can't fail!

The new dawn arises,
the wind it drives west,
'Twill help them sail out
on their wild treasure quest.
The quayside is bustling,
the cargo is stored,
Our captain's excited
now all are aboard.

His little dog Rufus
will not stop his barking,
The crew keep on singing
and playing and larking.
They sharpen their cutlass
and polish their gun,
They aim to be headed,
where treasure is won!

The harbour's behind
as they peer out to sea,
They wait for the order
to set the ship free.
Although 'tis a way
and the journey be rough,
Wee Rufus now barks out
a loud hearty woof!

WEIGH THE ANCHOR!
The bosun he yells!
And up it will come
with some barnacle shells.
It's time to set sail,
leave their loved ones behind,
If riches brought back,
surely no-one will mind!

Pet seagull called Squawk
is named just how he talks,
Old Bligh understands
all the words what he crawks!
Pet Hilary the cat,
is brought in for some luck,
All rats live in fear,
for they know of her pluck.

The tall wooden mast,
holds the flag to the sky,
A skull with two crossbones
speaks menace up high.
It's named Jolly Roger
but fearsome once seen,
By sailors at sea
or a king or a queen.

Young Roger the lad who helps clean the deck floors,
Gets pats on the head as he does the hard chores.
It's hard being a cabin boy, working on ship,
But for all his hard effort he gets a free trip.

At sea on the journey the crew sing their songs,
To boast about crimes and wild tales of their wrongs.
Whilst others they sing, the bosun plays fiddle,
He does a fine jig and a hey-diddle-diddle.

Since sailing at sea for well over one week,
They finally spy tropic isles that they seek.
It's time for the cap'n to walk his own plank,
The last man to do it, got pushed off and sank.

Our Bligh skips on by and jumps off for the show,
And lands in a craft, that lies bobbing below.
But just as he starts to row off in his boat,
He finds that he stares at a rather large throat!

A dart of a map, he throws up to the hatch,
Rowena leans out but she just cannot catch.
Whilst shouting out loud and her face full of fear
Into the shark's mouth, she sees Bligh disappear.

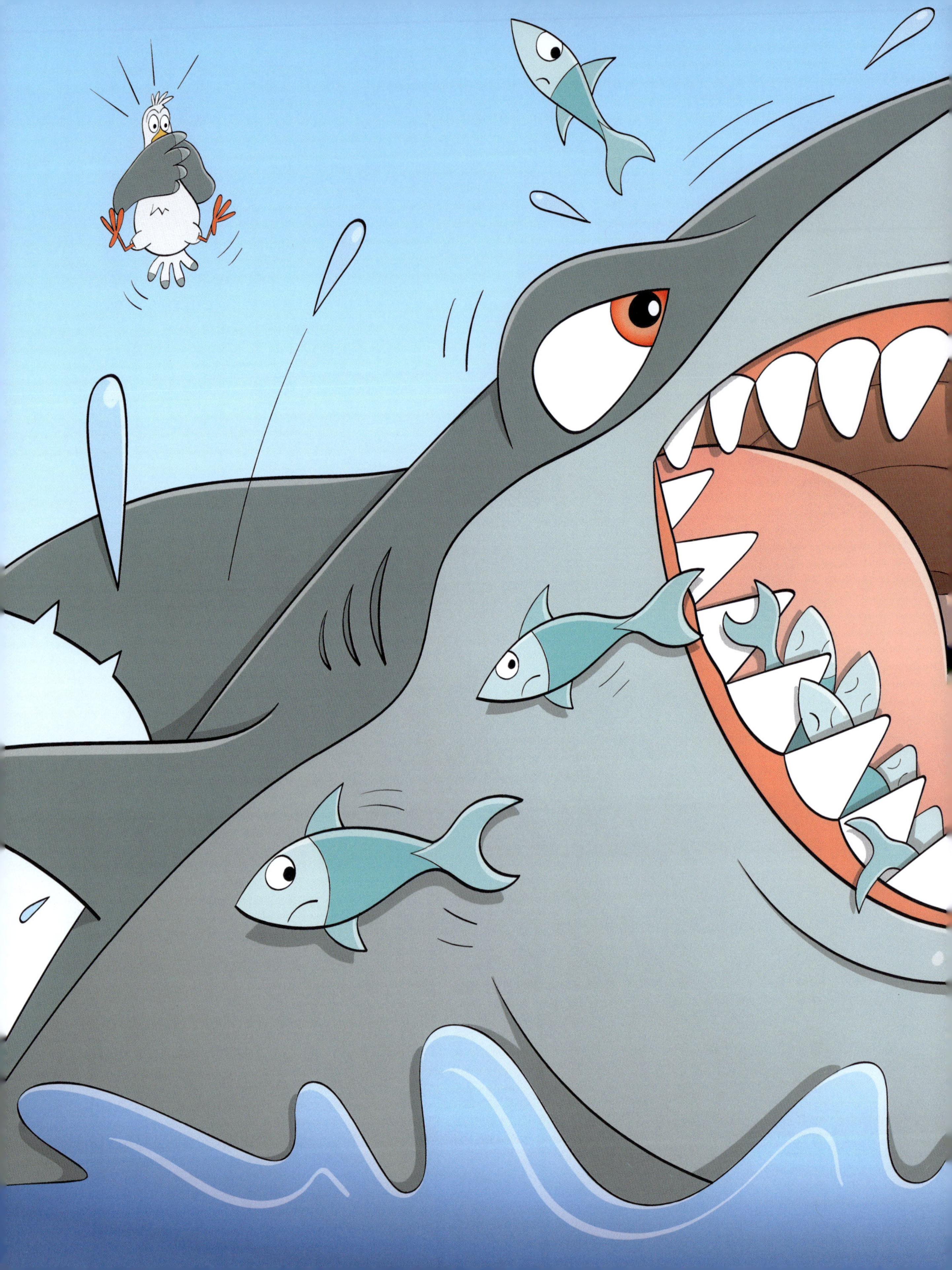

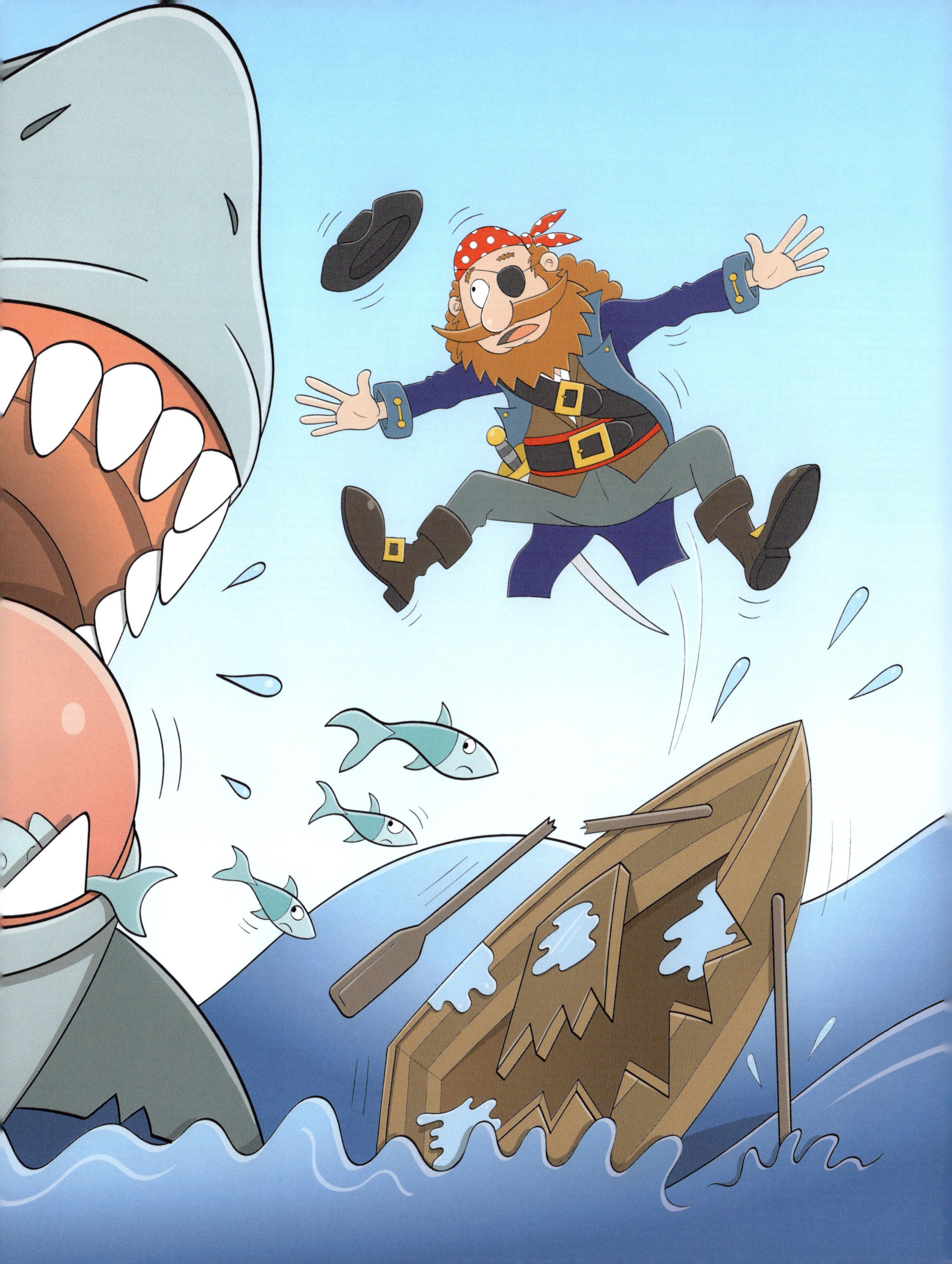

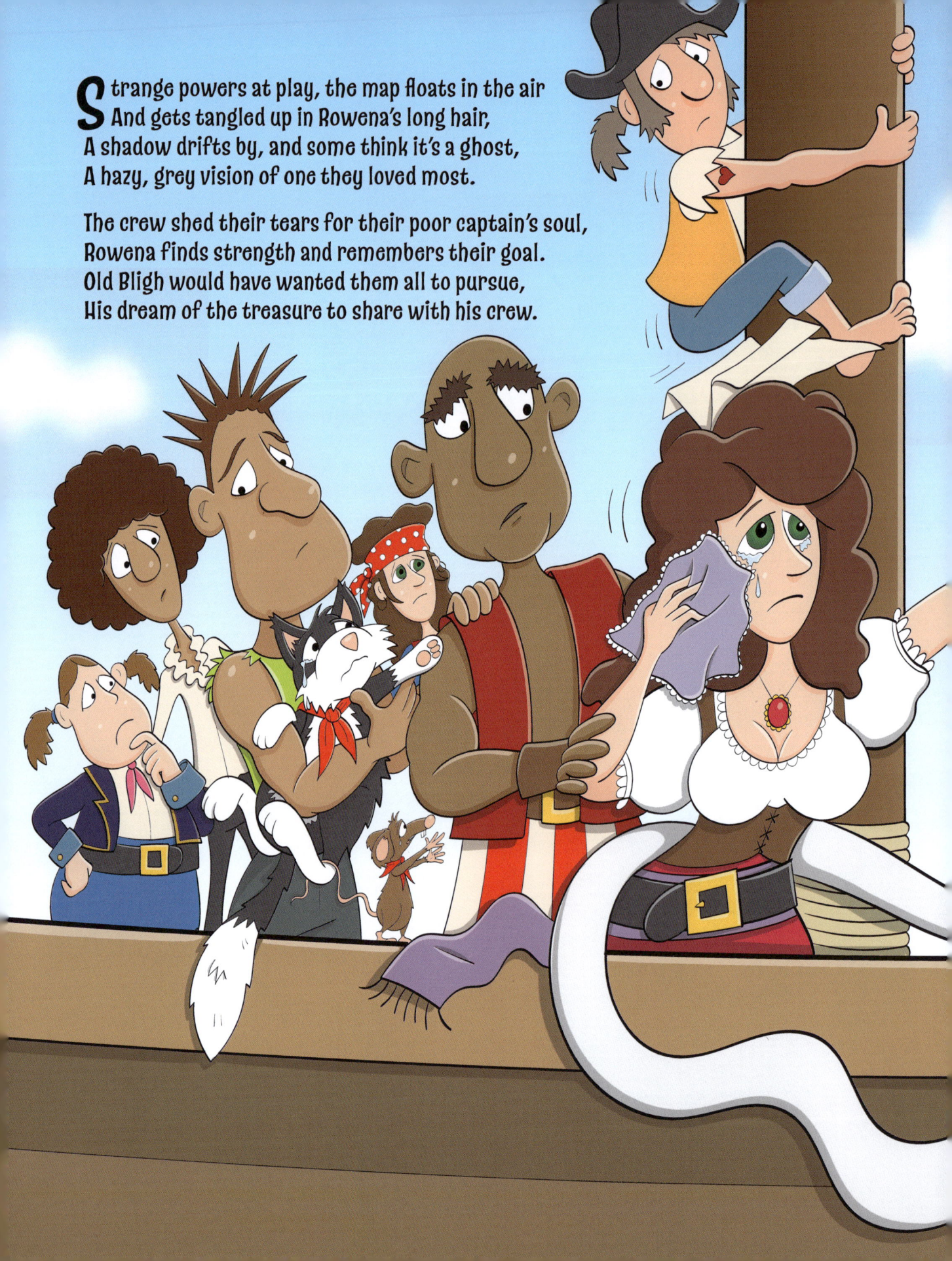

Strange powers at play, the map floats in the air
And gets tangled up in Rowena's long hair,
A shadow drifts by, and some think it's a ghost,
A hazy, grey vision of one they loved most.

The crew shed their tears for their poor captain's soul,
Rowena finds strength and remembers their goal.
Old Bligh would have wanted them all to pursue,
His dream of the treasure to share with his crew.

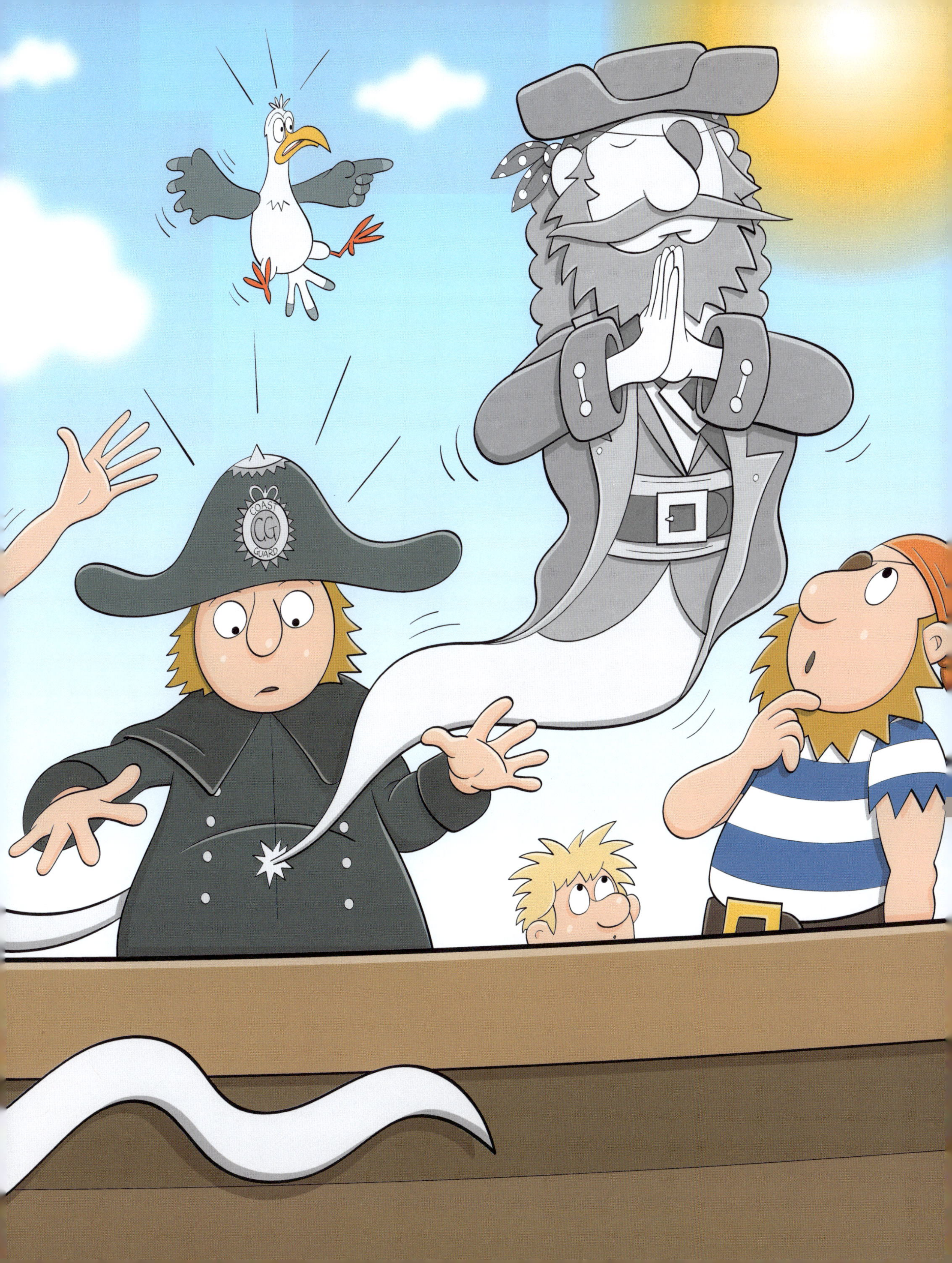
COAST
CG
GUARD

So onwards it be,
to find treasure that's buried,
They jump in small boats,
to the island be ferried.

The ship has dropped anchor, the crew's now ashore,
The bosun takes charge and he comes to the fore.
He looks at the map and then circles the cross
They can't get this wrong or 'twill be their sad loss.

Some ten paces forward, then ten paces right,
A further five forward, it should be in sight.
A palm tree with coconuts growing aplenty,
One step to the left and then forward a-twenty.

So, when they get there, where X marks the spot,
Somewhere down beneath, is there treasure, or not?
Our Rufus is sniffing, starts digging for bones,
Then gives out a yelp when he just brings up stones.

"But wait, what is this?!" cries the bosun with glee,
His eyes, they light up, as he grins happily.
There sat 'neath the stones be an old wooden chest,
And under the lid be a right treasure fest!

Spilled out on the sand there be wonders galore,
Small trinkets, gold coins and some jewellery and more.
Unknown to them all, lies a traitor in wait,
Guess who it might be, this one treacherous mate?

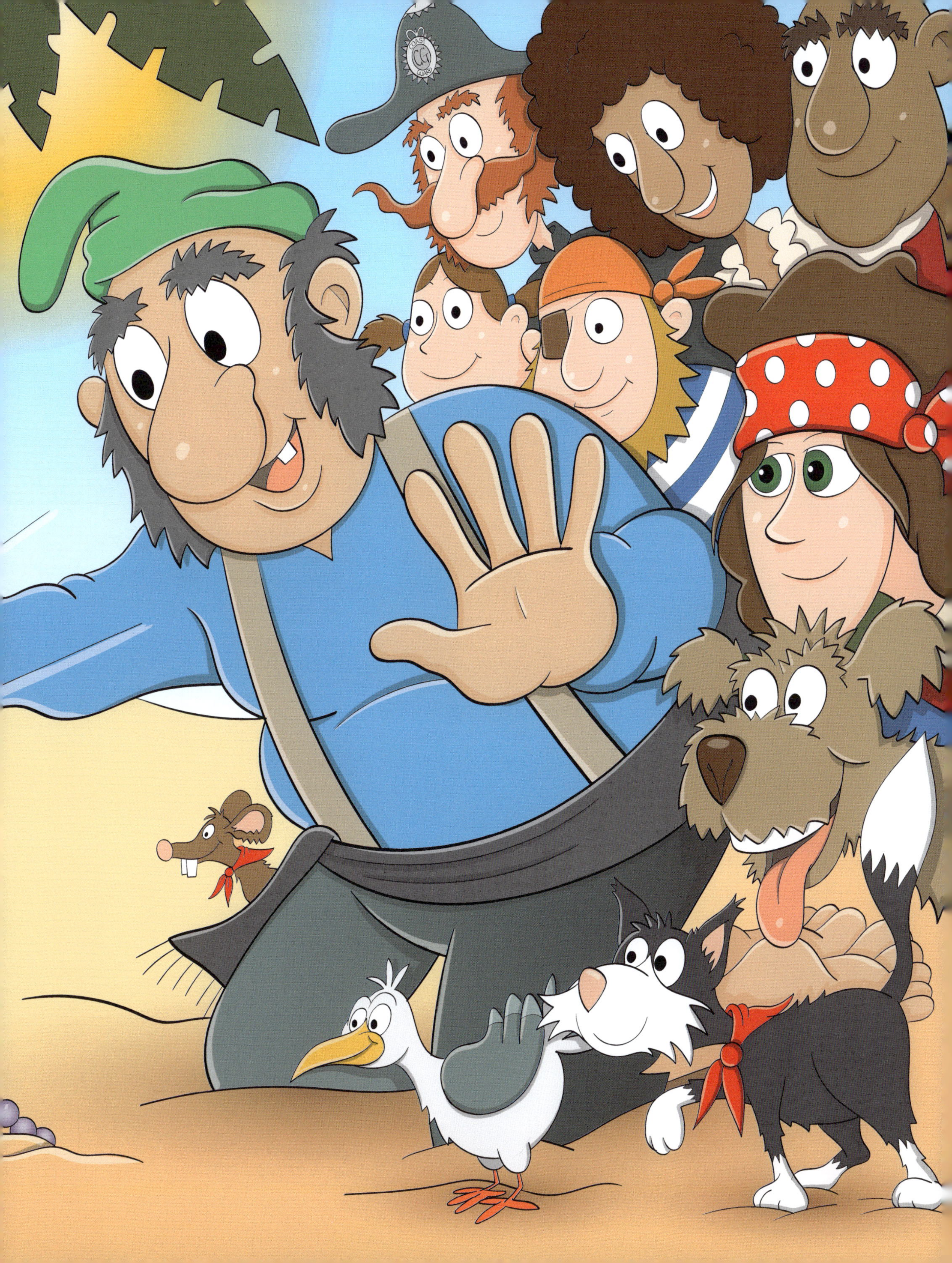

Bad Crab grabbed young Bets, and with venom he said,
to give him that treasure or she'll end up dead.
With Bets in a pickle, a hostage she be,
Who'll save this here day by a-settin' 'er free?

In flying and diving comes Squawk as he swoops,
Then onto Crab's head, this brave seagull poops.

SQUAWK!

Distracted by this, Crab then loses his grip,
He stumbles right over and so starts to trip.

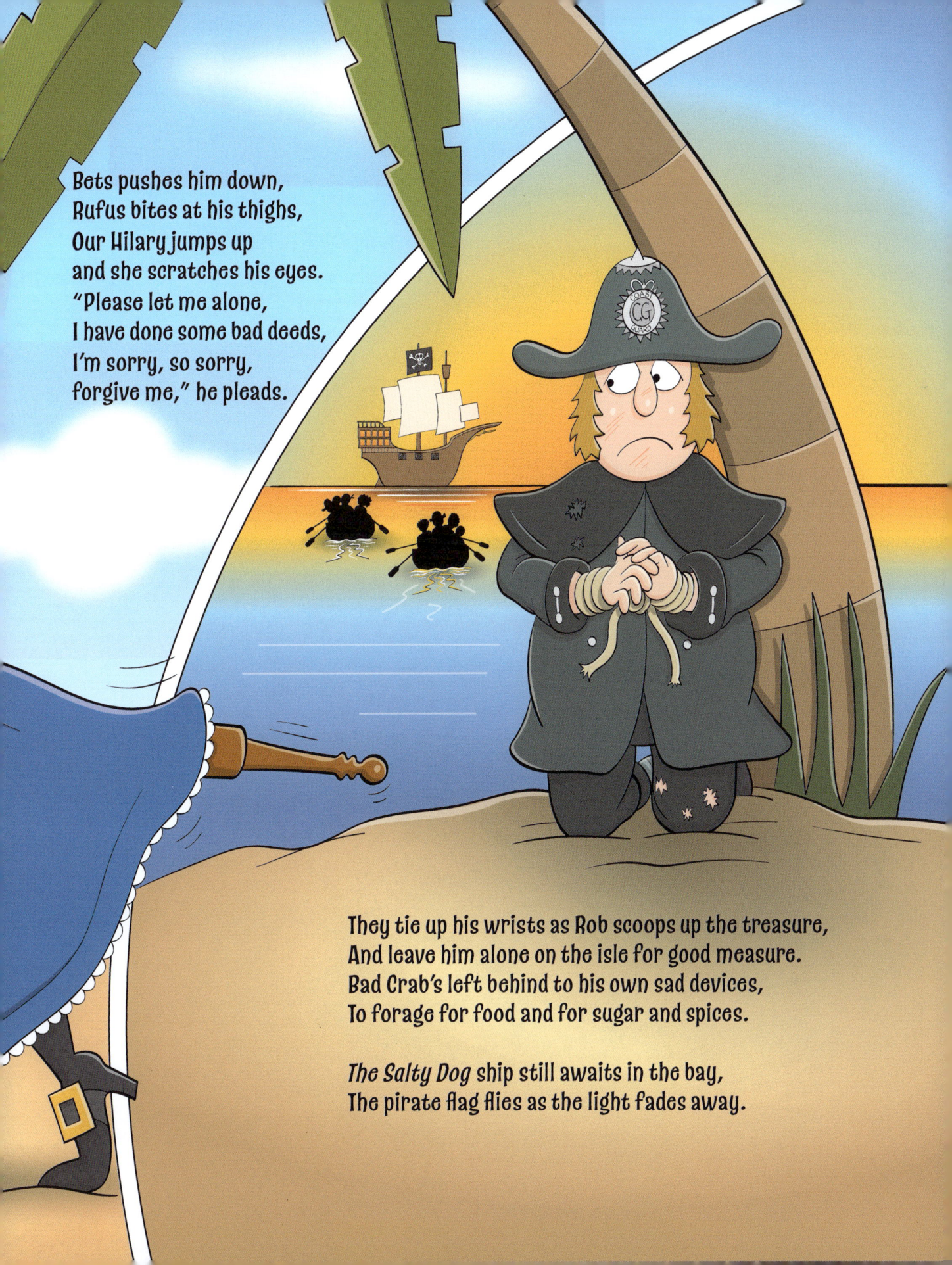

Bets pushes him down,
Rufus bites at his thighs,
Our Hilary jumps up
and she scratches his eyes.
"Please let me alone,
I have done some bad deeds,
I'm sorry, so sorry,
forgive me," he pleads.

They tie up his wrists as Rob scoops up the treasure,
And leave him alone on the isle for good measure.
Bad Crab's left behind to his own sad devices,
To forage for food and for sugar and spices.

The Salty Dog ship still awaits in the bay,
The pirate flag flies as the light fades away.

A figure is standing, it's manning the wheel.
They all stare in wonder, this cannot be real?
Rowena's so happy,
she cries out for joy,
She's found her true love,
her brave cap'n, her boy!

He'd wriggled and jiggled
and made the shark sick,
Rejected, ejected,
swam off with a kick!
His lungs were a-burstin',
he came up for air,
With seaweed and remnants
of fish in his hair.

He surfaced but found that his ship had sailed on,
No doubt with all thinking their captain had gone.
His clothes torn to shreds and his hat ripped up too,
He came to his senses and knew what to do!

A turtle swam by, and he asked for a lift,
They swam a few miles then he started to drift,
Toward his own ship, but no crew were on board,
He'd wait on the deck; they'd return with the hoard!

He hugs fair Rowena, a kiss he bestows,
Gets down on one knee and he starts to propose.
She kisses him back, says of course she'll accept,
Her love is so strong and no secret she's kept.

So soon there will be a big wedding at sea,
Where pirates rejoice and behave merrily!
A reading from Bosun Bill's big book of vows
A shindig for pirates, a party that wows!

The coastguards, one down, can't return to a job,
But Evans don't care, he belongs to this mob.
The sergeant loves Bets and he dreams of a wife,
She might just say no but he's pirate for life!

It's time to go home now the treasure's been found,
And into the sunset they sail safe and sound.

The End

Also by Dave Whittle

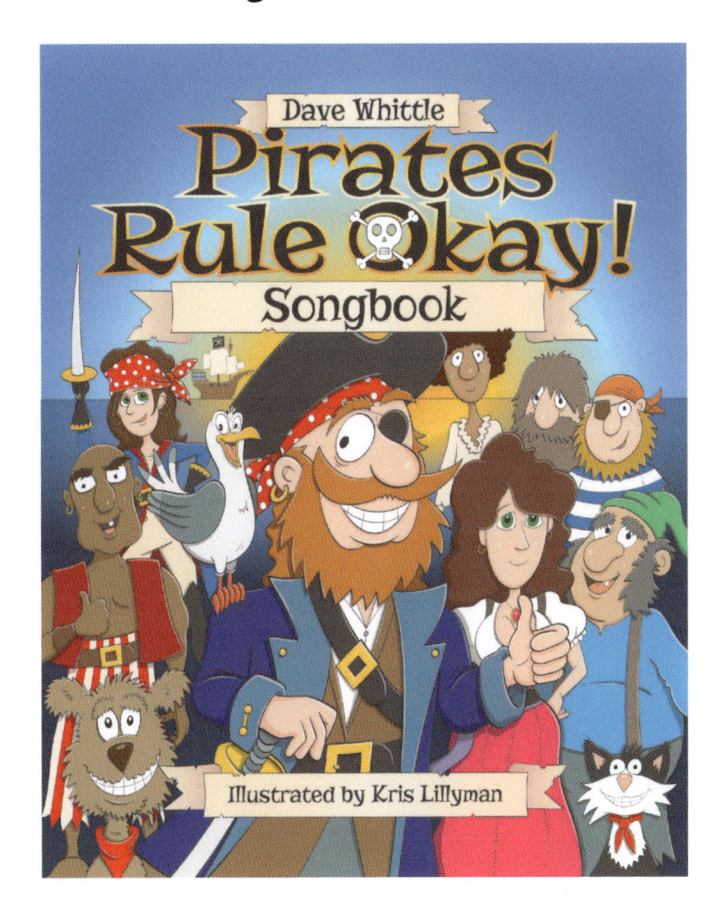

Check out www.piratesruleok.com for further details

Printed in Great Britain
by Amazon